FEROCIOUS FIGHTING ANIMALS

HYENAS

Julia J. Quinlan

PowerKiDS
press™

New York

Published in 2013 by The Rosen Publishing Group, Inc.
29 East 21st Street, New York, NY 10010

First Edition

Editor: Amelie von Zumbusch
Book Design: Andrew Povolny

Photo Credits: Cover Kim Wolhuter/National Geographic/Getty Images; p. 4 Achim Mittler, Frankfurt am Main/Flickr/Getty Images; p. 5 Tom Brakefield/Stockbyte/Thinkstock; p. 6 Mattias Klum/National Geographic/Getty Images; pp. 7 (bottom), 7 (top), 8 iStockphoto/Thinkstock; p. 9 Doug Cheeseman/Oxford Scientific/Getty Images; pp. 10–11 Miguel Sanz/Flickr/Getty Images; pp. 12–13 Nigel Dennis/Gallo Images/Getty Images; p. 14 Gregory MD./Photo Researchers/Getty Images; p. 15 Ingram Publishing/Thinkstock.com; pp. 16–17 Anan Kaewkhammul/Shutterstock.com; p. 18 Nigel J Dennis/Photo Researchers/Getty Images; p. 19 Beverly Joubert/National Geographic/Getty Images; p. 20 Gunter Ziesler/Peter Arnold/Getty Images; p. 21 Tim Jackson/Oxford Scientific/Getty Images; p. 22 Andrew Holt/Photographer's Choice/Getty Images.

Library of Congress Cataloging-in-Publication Data

Quinlan, Julia J.
  Hyenas / by Julia J. Quinlan. — 1st ed.
      p. cm. — (Ferocious fighting animals)
  Includes index.
  ISBN 978-1-4488-9673-8 (library binding) — ISBN 978-1-4488-9804-6 (pbk.) —
  ISBN 978-1-4488-9805-3 (6-pack)
  1. Hyenas—Juvenile literature. I. Title.
  QL737.C24Q46 2013
  599.74'3—dc23
                                    2012027663

Manufactured in the United States of America

CPSIA Compliance Information: Batch #W13PK5: For Further Information contact Rosen Publishing, New York, New York at 1-800-237-9932

CONTENTS

MEET THE HYENA

Hyenas are fast animals with powerful jaws. They can defend themselves against animals that are much bigger than they are. Some hyenas gang up to fight other animals. Hyenas are vicious fighters and have been known to attack people.

Spotted hyenas, such as this one, sometimes attack farm animals. They mostly attack sheep but also go after cattle and donkeys.

There are three **species** known as hyenas. They are the spotted hyena, the brown hyena, and the striped hyena. Each species looks and acts a bit differently. Along with an animal called the aardwolf, these species make up the hyena **family**. Hyenas share **traits** with both cats and dogs, but their closest relatives are mongooses and meerkats.

Aardwolves live in eastern and southern Africa. They are smaller and shyer than hyenas. Insects are their main food.

SPOTTED, STRIPED, OR BROWN?

Every species of hyena is found in Africa. Striped hyenas also live in the Middle East and other parts of Asia.

Brown hyenas have long, coarse brown fur. They have bushy tails and long, pointed ears. As all hyenas do, they have long front legs and short back legs.

Brown hyenas are most common along the southwestern coast of Africa and in Africa's Kalahari Desert.

Striped hyenas can be gray, brown, or golden yellow. They have black stripes, similar to a zebra's. They can weigh as much as 121 pounds (55 kg).

A striped hyena's tail can be up to 14 inches (35 cm) long.

Spotted hyenas have light brown fur with dark brown spots. They are the biggest hyenas. They have rounded ears and short, coarse fur.

It is hard to tell male and female spotted hyenas apart. Females tend to be bigger, though.

GROWING UP

Female hyenas give birth to between one and four cubs at a time. Hyena cubs drink their mothers' milk. After a month or so, they also eat meat.

Spotted hyenas are born with their eyes open and with some of their teeth. Striped hyenas are born blind. Their eyes open after about a week.

Spotted hyena cubs, like this one, are born with dark fur. Their fur grows lighter as they age.

Striped hyena cubs can be born at any time of year but are most commonly born at times when there is plenty of food to eat.

Striped hyena mothers raise their cubs alone. Brown hyena cubs are cared for by their whole **clan**, or group. Spotted hyenas are often born in special dens away from the rest of their clan. They join the clan den when they are a few weeks old.

HUNGRY SPOTTED HYENAS

Spotted hyenas are not picky eaters. They eat **mammals**, birds, fish, and reptiles. They also eat garbage left behind by people and the **dung** of other animals. Usually, spotted hyenas hunt their prey and kill it themselves. Sometimes they hunt in groups of two to five. They will also eat animals that have been killed by other predators or have died from other causes.

Spotted hyenas have very strong jaws and sharp teeth that they use to kill their prey. They are fast runners. When hunting in groups, hyenas will run together and surround their prey before attacking it.

A spotted hyena can eat up to 40 pounds (18 kg) of food in one sitting.

FEROCIOUS HYENAS

Spotted hyenas are tough! They fight fiercely to defend or steal kills. Their jaws crush bones easily. Special fluids in their stomachs let them digest bones, hair, skin, and teeth. Even cubs are ferocious! They often kill weaker cubs.

WORKING TOGETHER

Spotted hyena clans can be very large. They may have as many as 90 hyenas. The females are the heads of the clan. Hyenas fight with each other for **dominance** over the clan. The female that wins the most fights is the clan's leader. The female hyena that has lost the most fights is still above the male hyena that has won the most fights.

Spotted hyenas often share kills with the rest of their clan.

Spotted hyenas start fighting for dominance when they are cubs.

Spotted hyenas are known for making a sound that sounds just like laughter. In fact, hyenas make many sounds. Each sound means something different. Less powerful hyenas make giggling sounds when faced with dominant clan members.

STRIPED HYENAS

Striped hyenas **scavenge** more than they hunt. They eat mostly animals that were killed by other predators, such as spotted hyenas and lions. Vegetables, fruits, and waste left by humans are also part of their diet. Striped hyenas sometimes hunt smaller animals. They usually hunt or scavenge at night.

Striped hyenas don't live in very large groups. At most, four hyenas will live together. They almost always scavenge and hunt alone. Mother hyenas will sometimes look for food with their cubs. Striped hyenas are quieter than other hyena species. Cubs make noises, but adults are mostly silent.

Striped hyenas hear very well. They also have good senses of smell and sight.

BROWN HYENAS

Brown hyenas scavenge for food alone and at night. Besides dead animals, brown hyenas also eat fruit, birds' eggs, and insects. Rarely, they will kill and eat a small animal. Brown hyenas live in small clans that are usually made up of one female and her cubs or a couple of females and their cubs. Male hyenas will either go off on their own, remain with the clan they grew up with, or join a new clan.

Brown hyenas that live along the southwest coast of Africa eat baby seals. They also eat ocean animals that wash up onshore.

When they have extra food, brown hyenas will sometimes hide it to eat later.

Brown hyenas are generally quiet unless they are fighting. All hyenas have **scent glands**. Brown hyenas use these glands to communicate with other hyenas. They leave their scent in different places.

FIGHTING HYENAS

Spotted hyenas compete with lions, leopards, and cheetahs for food. Even though lions are larger than spotted hyenas, the hyenas can sometimes fight off a lion if enough of their clan is present. Spotted hyenas are more evenly matched with cheetahs and leopards. Spotted hyenas can beat striped hyenas and brown hyenas in fights. These smaller hyenas are no match for lions either.

This group of hyenas is attacking several lions that are eating a warthog.

Here, a brown hyena chases away a group of jackals from a dead wildebeest. Like brown hyenas, jackals often scavenge for food.

Hyenas have powerful jaws, teeth, and claws that they can use in a fight. For example, the pressure of an adult striped hyena's bite can be up to 800 pounds per square inch (56 kg/sq cm).

PROTECTING HYENAS

Hyenas and humans do not have a very good relationship. Many farmers dislike hyenas because they kill and eat **livestock**. Lately, more people have moved into areas where hyenas live. This causes problems between people and hyenas. People poison, trap, and shoot hyenas.

In some areas, certain hyena species are threatened and even **endangered**. This is mainly because there is not enough land for them to live on. Luckily, there are many people and groups that work to **protect** hyenas.

Many countries have set aside land for hyenas and other wild animals. This spotted hyena is in Kruger National Park, in South Africa.

GLOSSARY

clan (KLAN) A group of animals that live together.

dominance (DAH-mih-nunts) Ruling over or standing out above all others.

dung (DUNG) Animal waste.

endangered (in-DAYN-jerd) In danger of no longer existing.

family (FAM-lee) The scientific name for a large group of plants or animals that are alike in some ways.

livestock (LYV-stok) Animals raised by people.

mammals (MA-mulz) Warm-blooded animals that have backbones and hair, breathe air, and feed milk to their young.

protect (pruh-TEKT) To keep safe.

scavenge (SKA-venj) To find and eat dead things.

scent glands (SENT GLANDZ) Body parts that make a smell that animals use to mark their land.

species (SPEE-sheez) One kind of living thing. All people are one species.

traits (TRAYTS) Features that make an individual special.

INDEX

WEBSITES

Due to the changing nature of Internet links, PowerKids Press has developed an online list of websites related to the subject of this book. This site is updated regularly. Please use this link to access the list: www.powerkidslinks.com/ffa/hyen/